Bernadette Cuxart

spooky
characters

BARRON'S

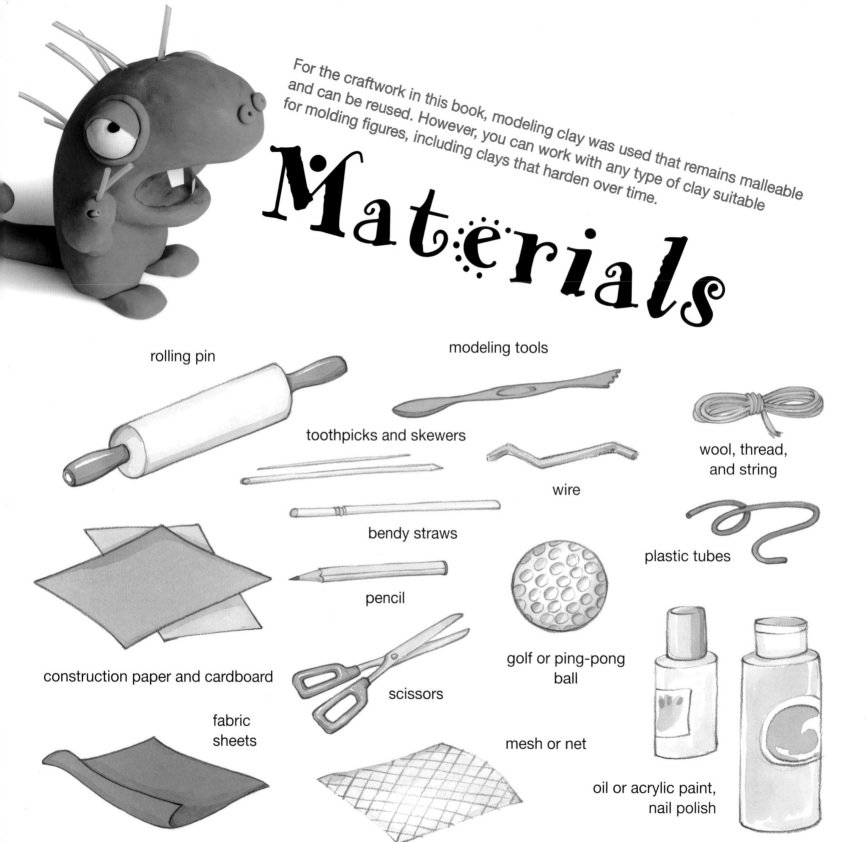

For the craftwork in this book, modeling clay was used that remains malleable and can be reused. However, you can work with any type of clay suitable for molding figures, including clays that harden over time.

Materials

rolling pin

modeling tools

toothpicks and skewers

wool, thread, and string

wire

bendy straws

plastic tubes

pencil

construction paper and cardboard

golf or ping-pong ball

scissors

fabric sheets

mesh or net

oil or acrylic paint, nail polish

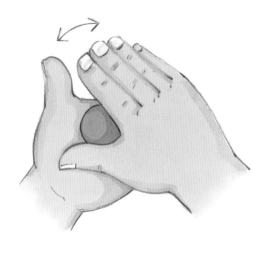

BALLS

Mold a piece of modeling clay in the palms of your hands until it forms a sphere.

Basic techniques

SAUSAGES

If you roll a piece of modeling clay on a table with your fingers together, it will form a sausage shape. Alter the pressure you apply depending on the shape and thickness you want.

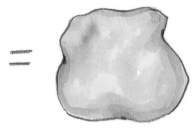

MIXING COLORS

You can create new colors by mixing modeling clay. If you mix them slightly, you will have some veined dough with which you can obtain very interesting effects. If you mix them more, you will obtain a new color.

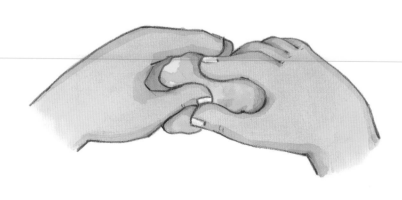

SHEETS AND TOOTHPICK SHAPES

To make flat figures, roll some modeling clay out on some plastic or paper, to prevent it from sticking to the table. Start from a ball, and flatten it with a rolling pin. To cut shapes out from a sheet, use a toothpick: First mark the shapes and then cut until they come out.

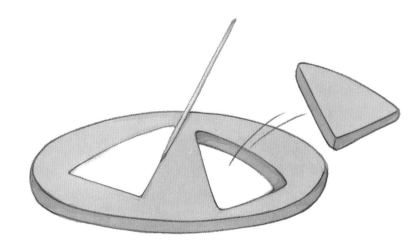

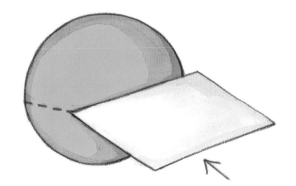

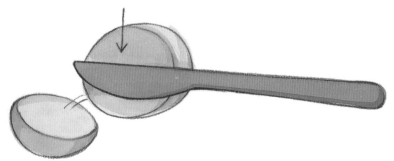

CUTTING

For cutting modeling clay, in addition to specific tools, you can use thread held tightly between your fingers or a piece of cardboard.

RESISTANT JOINS

Use pieces of toothpick to join together parts that need to be strong. Then smooth the join with your fingers.

PAINT

Modeling clay can be painted with runny oil or acrylic paint. Nail polish also looks very good.

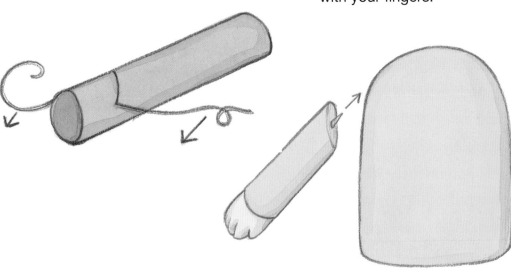

SIMPLE HANDS

Cut the tip off a ball and flatten it a little. Mark the fingers with the help of a toothpick. To finish, stick the hand onto its corresponding arm with a piece of toothpick.

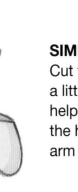

TEXTURES

You can create textures using many different materials. For example, by pressing the bend of a flexible straw on the modeling clay, you can mark scars. Or by pressing with some mesh, you can simulate weave and patches, etc.

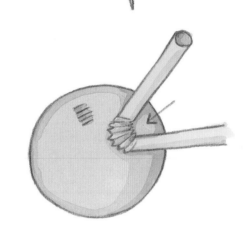

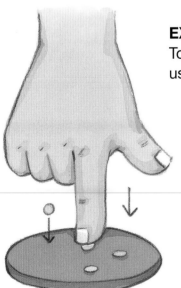

EXTRAS

To add features like moles, you can use flattened balls and buttons, etc.

FACES

The basics of a face are simple. A little ball for the nose. A stripe made with a toothpick for the mouth (or with a skewer if you want it to be bigger). The ears are made from half a flattened ball each. And for the eyes, you have to make little balls and flatten them one over the other, smaller each time. You can add a white one at the end, to simulate a shine.

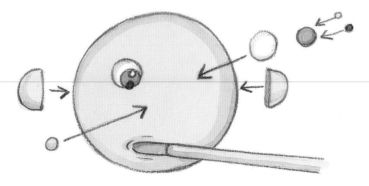

Pumpkin

1. Cover a golf or ping-pong ball with a 1 cm thick layer of orange modeling clay. You should end up with a sphere.

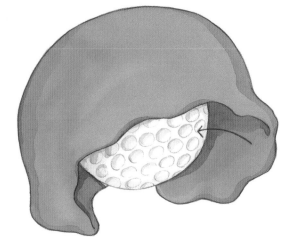

2. Cut the sphere in half and remove the ball.

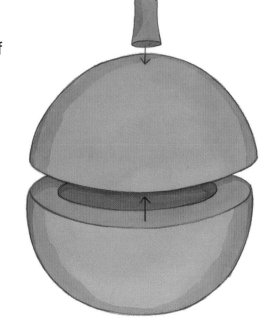

3. Join the two halves back together and smooth the joint. Stick a small cylinder at the top, which will be the stalk.

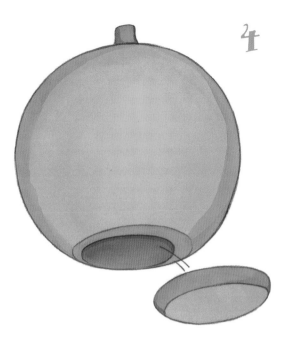

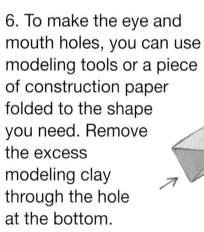

4. Make a hole in the bottom. You can place your finger inside to strengthen the joint between the two halves.

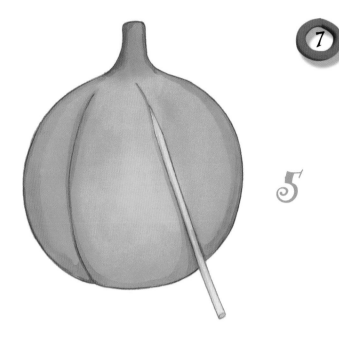

5. Mark the lines with a skewer. Finish off the shapes with your fingers.

6. To make the eye and mouth holes, you can use modeling tools or a piece of construction paper folded to the shape you need. Remove the excess modeling clay through the hole at the bottom.

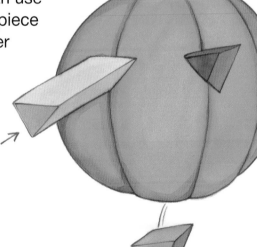

Halloween

Pumpkins look like heads. At Halloween, they are emptied and a candle is placed inside. When they are lit, they are very scary...

Bat

1. We need two large balls for the head and body. With two smaller balls, we will make the thighs. Model a cone for the tail.

1

Blind

Bats sleep upside down during the day and fly at night. As they are very short-sighted, they get their bearings thanks to sound waves. Most of them usually eat insects.

2

2. Stick a little ball in the middle of the face. Mark the mouth with a toothpick and stick two white construction paper triangles underneath. For the eyes, make two small holes with a sharp pencil.

3

3. Stick the head onto the body with a piece of toothpick. The ears are made from construction paper (you will find the patterns on p. 35).

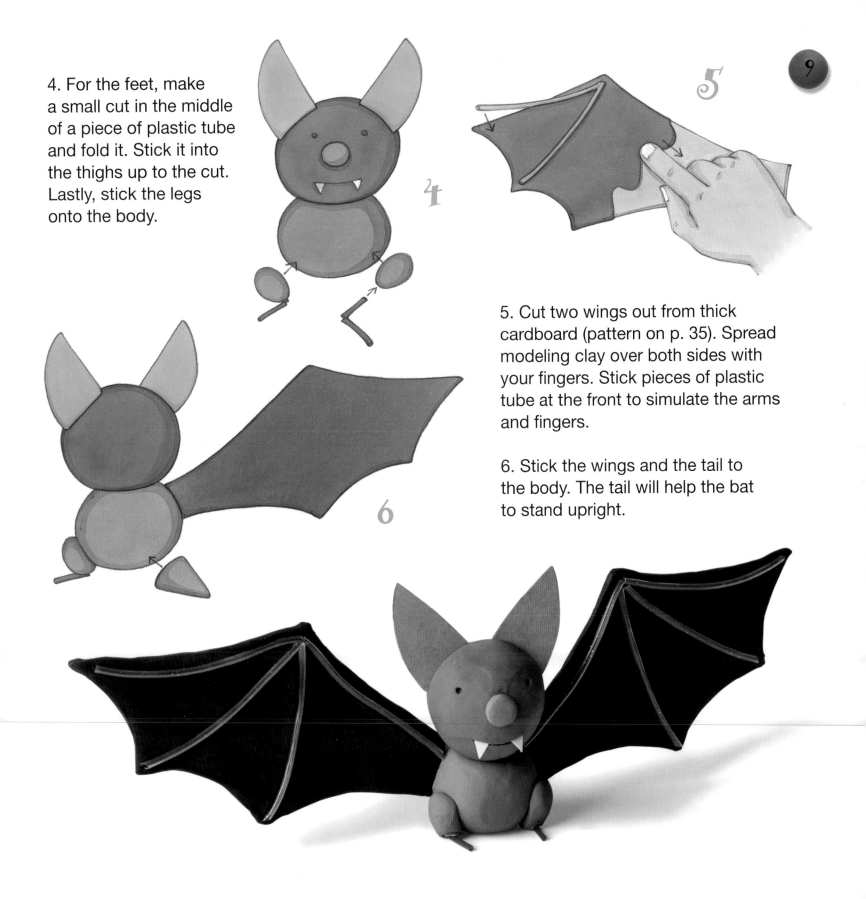

4. For the feet, make a small cut in the middle of a piece of plastic tube and fold it. Stick it into the thighs up to the cut. Lastly, stick the legs onto the body.

5. Cut two wings out from thick cardboard (pattern on p. 35). Spread modeling clay over both sides with your fingers. Stick pieces of plastic tube at the front to simulate the arms and fingers.

6. Stick the wings and the tail to the body. The tail will help the bat to stand upright.

Ghost

1. Assemble the internal structure: a cylinder that is wider at the base, a ball for the head, and two raised sausages for the arms. Join them all together with pieces of toothpick.

1

2

2. Prepare a white sheet 3–4 mm thick, large enough to cover the structure.

3

3. Give it the form of a sheet, using your fingers. Try to define the head and arms well. Mark some folds at the bottom. To finish, stick on three little black balls to simulate the eye and mouth holes.

Spider

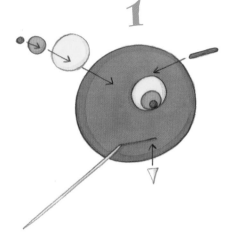

1

2

1. Model a ball for the head. First make the eyes from two yellow balls, then medium-sized ones, and tiny ones at the end. Make some modeling clay eyebrows to give it an unfriendly expression…
Mark the ball with a toothpick and stick some construction paper fangs inside.

2. Cut some wool into very small pieces and cover the ball in it to give it a hairy body.

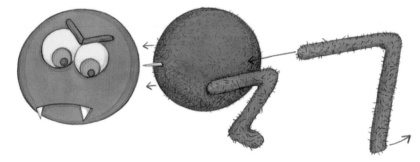

3

3. Join the two balls together with a piece of toothpick. Stick pieces of pipe cleaner into the body, and fold them so that they support your spider well.

Lying in wait

Many people are afraid of large hairy spiders. If you find a spider's web, there might be one nearby…

Vampire

1. The body is made from a white cylinder rounded at the top, and the arms are made from sausages the same color. Make the legs from dark modeling clay.

2. Model and stick the hands (see p. 5) from a cold color. Join the arms to the body, smoothing out the joins.

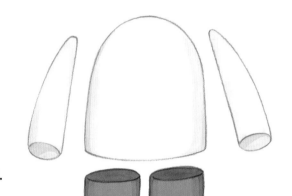

Creatures of the night

Just like bats, vampires sleep during the day. At night, they go out in search of food and feed on the blood they suck from their victims. They leave no reflection in mirrors. They cannot bear garlic or crosses.

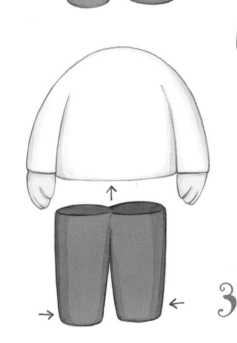

3. Join the legs together, giving them the shape of pants, and stick them onto the body.

4. Mark a line in the middle of the shirt and add two white triangles cut out from a sheet of modeling clay. To make the shoes, model a ball into a teardrop shape and cut it in half. Stick the halves onto the pants.

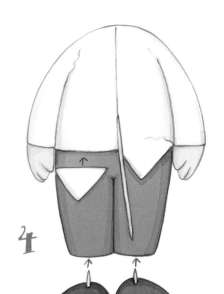

5. Model the head using the same color as the hands. Make the face (see p. 5). Cut out two fangs from construction paper and stick them onto the mouth. Now you just have to paint the hair.

6

6. Stick the head onto the shoulders. Cut out a piece of black fabric for the cloak (use the pattern on p. 35). Tie it around the neck with a piece of ribbon.

Witch

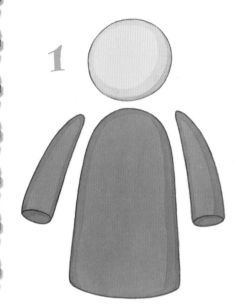

1. Model a thick cylinder and round it off at the top. With the same color modeling clay, make the sausages for the arms. A skin-colored ball will be the head.

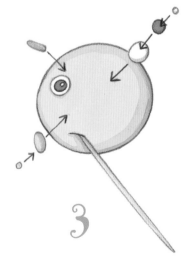

2. Model the hands (see p. 5). Join the arms to the body. Model the boots and stick them on, too.

3. Now make the face (see p. 5). Mark the mouth with a toothpick and add a modeling clay tooth. Don't forget the nose with a wart! You can give it color with red chalk dust and a paintbrush.

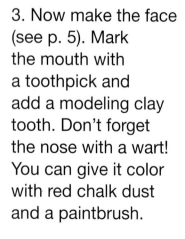

4. Cut strips of wool for the hair. Tie them in the middle, stick them onto the head with a pin, and arrange the hair. Flatten a small ball on the shoulders and stick the head on it with a piece of toothpick.

5. Make a sheet and cut out the pattern on p. 35 with a toothpick. Roll it into a cone and smooth the join. Lift up the brim and you have the witch's hat.

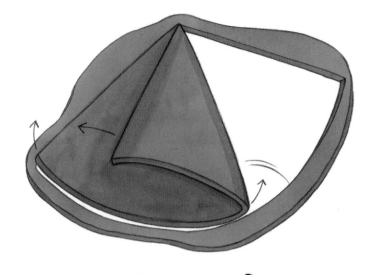

5

6

6. Put it on her and tilt the tip. Decorate it with a flattened sausage in a different color. To make the broom, tie some unraveled string to a piece of skewer and place it in her hands. Give shape to the dress.

The power of magic

If a witch gives you a potion, don't drink it! It might turn you into a toad or you might even disappear... Witches know a lot of spells.

Monster

1. Model a rounded cylinder thicker on one side and flatter and thinner on the other. Bend it, trying to make sure that it stands up well. Open a large mouth with a pencil.

2. Paint the inside of the mouth with acrylic paint. Once it is dry, stick in two construction paper teeth.

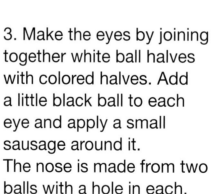

3. Make the eyes by joining together white ball halves with colored halves. Add a little black ball to each eye and apply a small sausage around it. The nose is made from two balls with a hole in each.

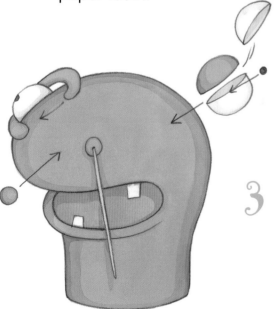

4. Join two sausages to the body and stick pieces of plastic tube into them for the fingers.

5. Now stick two pieces of modeling clay under the base: They will be the feet. Mark a little bridge between the feet with a pencil.

6. Finish off the monster with a curly tail, which will also help it to balance. Stick pieces of plastic tube into the back, like a crest.

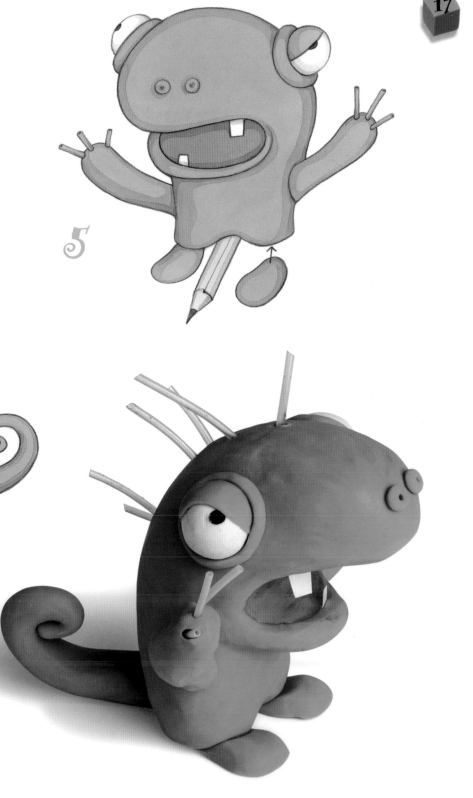

Many shapes and sizes

The monsters' job is to scare people, although they don't always manage to do so... There are many types, and you can find them in books, films, or in your worst nightmare! Imagine yours...

Mummy

1

1. A rounded cylinder for the body, a ball for the head, and four sausages for the limbs. It is all white, although you can make the hands and other parts from skin color.

2. Join the legs to the body with toothpicks, and model the ends in the shape of feet.

2

3

3. The arms should be held forward, to scare people… Mark the fingers with a toothpick.

4. Make two hollows in the face to place two yellow balls inside with two small black balls on top. Make the nose and mark the mouth with a skewer.

4

5. Strengthen the neck with a sausage and smooth it out. Cut out strips of paper (such as toilet paper) and wrap them around the mummy. Place a drop of glue on the start and end of each strip.

it's coming!

In ancient Egypt, corpses were wrapped in bandages and kept in sarcophaguses. How scary if they opened and walked out!

6. Wrap it well, leaving the eyes, mouth, and hands uncovered. Age the bandages by applying ochre chalk dust with a paintbrush. What an old mummy!

Black cat

1. We need a rounded sausage for the body, a ball for the head, and four sausages pointed at the ends for the legs, two thicker than the others.

2. To assemble the face, make the eyes from two flattened white balls and smaller ones on top. Use a small pyramid for the nose (well joined at the top) and two balls for the cheeks.

3. Finish the head with another pyramid underneath with a pink base, as if its mouth were open. Stick some construction paper triangles under the cheeks. Add the whiskers from nylon thread. And for the ears, spread modeling clay over some cardboard triangles and stick them in.

Color of the night

Black cats have a mysterious air that disturbs many people... Some even say that they bring bad luck. Did you know that they are the companion animals of many witches?

4. Smooth the join until it cannot be seen. Stick the head onto the body with a piece of toothpick and smooth the join underneath. Arch the body slightly.

5. Stick the four legs in with pieces of toothpick, the thicker ones at the back. Bend the ends slightly to make the foot shape.

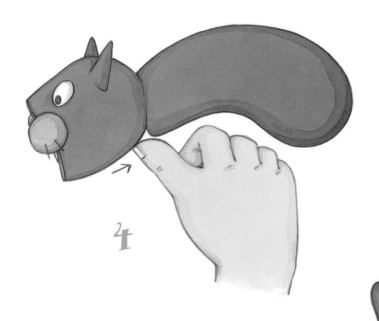

6. To finish, model a tail and stick it on with a piece of toothpick.

Ogre

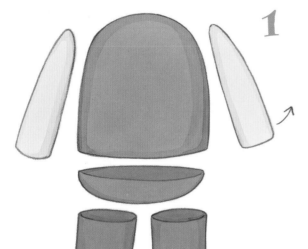

1. The body is a cylinder rounded at one end. Model the arms and legs with sausages, the latter much thicker. You will need half an oval for the pants top.

2. Join the legs to the pants top and smooth out the joins. Stick the pants onto the body.

3. Make the hands (see p. 5). Stick the arms onto the body with pieces of toothpick and bend one arm at the elbow. Stick and smooth a colored triangle onto each shoulder for it to look like a vest.

Run!

Ogres are large, gawky characters. They love scaring children, and in some stories they try to eat them!

4. Make some boots by sticking half ovals into the legs and adding a flat strip around the ankles. The belt can also be a flat strip, to which you can add a buckle made from a sausage.

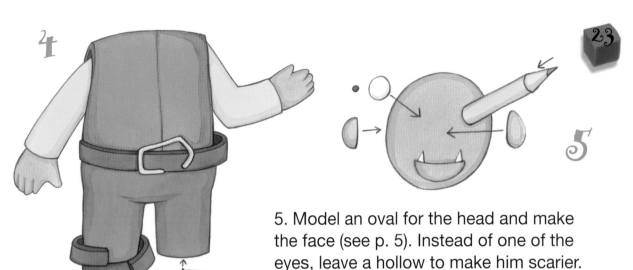

5. Model an oval for the head and make the face (see p. 5). Instead of one of the eyes, leave a hollow to make him scarier. Add the chin with a flattened half ball, smooth the joins and stick on some construction paper fangs.

6. To finish the face, you will need: Little balls for warts, little sausages for eyebrows, a bendy straw to mark the scars, and some pieces of plastic tube for the beard. Stick the head in at chest height so that he appears hunchbacked. Place a modeling clay club in his hand.

Skeleton

1. Model a skull by elongating a ball. Make two eyes and a nose with the two ends of a pencil. Mark the mouth with a piece of construction paper folded in a zigzag.

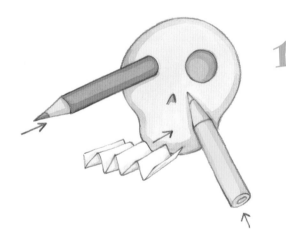

2. Model the shape of the hips as shown in the drawing and make a hole in the middle.

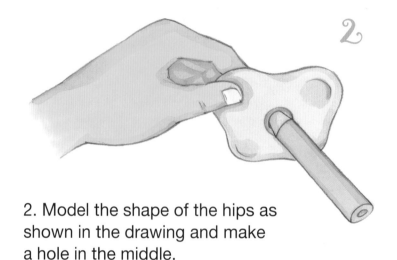

3. Paint a piece of skewer bone color and stick the head on one end and the hips on the other. Stick some sausages behind for the ribs.

4. The arms are toothpicks covered in modeling clay. The joints and the hands are little balls. Make the finger bones from plastic tubes and stick on the arms.

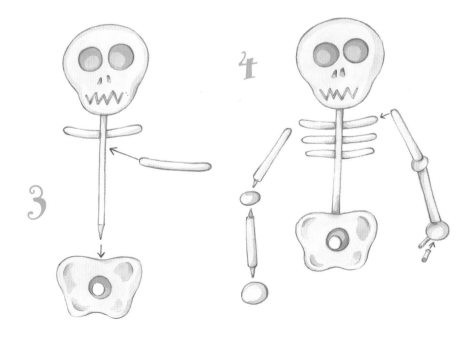

5. Follow the same process for the legs, using longer toothpicks. Join the legs to the bottom part of the hips.

6. Place your skeleton on a flat earth-colored base. You can add some modeling clay stones.

5

Boy or girl?

Archaeologists often find skeletons of people and animals that lived during other times.

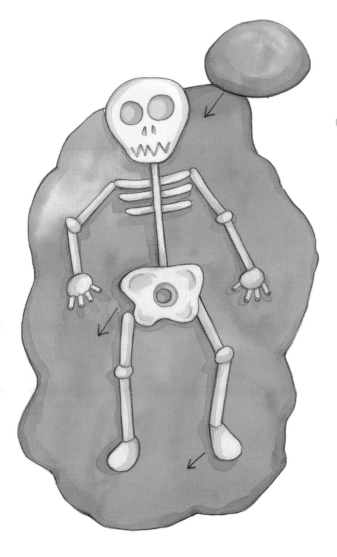

6

Jelly monster

1. Model a ball, banging it slightly to make a flat base. If you mix two colors, knead them slightly to be left with veins.

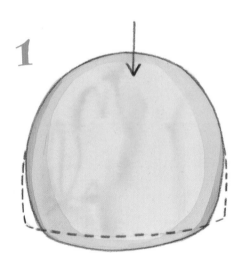

2. Spread the modeling clay downward with your finger to give it a jelly appearance.

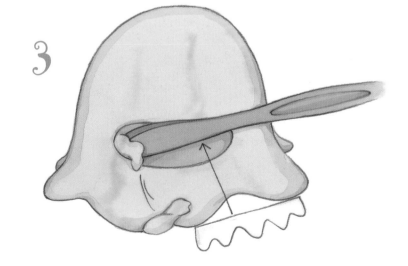

3. Open a large mouth with a modeling tool. Smooth it with your finger and stick some construction paper teeth inside.

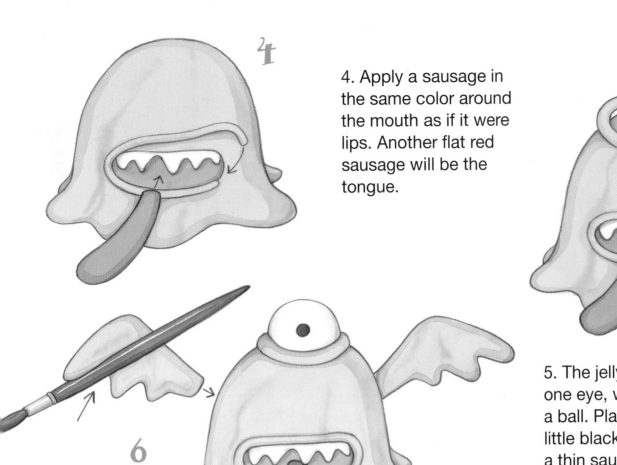

4. Apply a sausage in the same color around the mouth as if it were lips. Another flat red sausage will be the tongue.

5. The jelly monster only has one eye, which is made from half a ball. Place it on top and add a little black ball. Surround it with a thin sausage.

6. Model two winged arms with the help of a tool or a paintbrush. Stick one on each side of the monster and you've finished!

imagine monsters

Which monsters are scary? For example, are you scared by one that looks like jelly, can fly, and can stick onto your body?

Pirate

1

1. A rounded cylinder for the body, two pointed sausages for the arms, and a ball for the head. For the pants, use an oval and two sausages, one longer than the other.

2. Make the hand (see p. 5). On the other arm, we will give him a hook: a piece of wire stuck into a half ball. Join the arms to the body and smooth out the joins.

2

3. Join together the two sausages and the oval and smooth the joins. Stick on a boot and a strip around the long leg. For the "peg leg" use a skewer and half a ball.

3

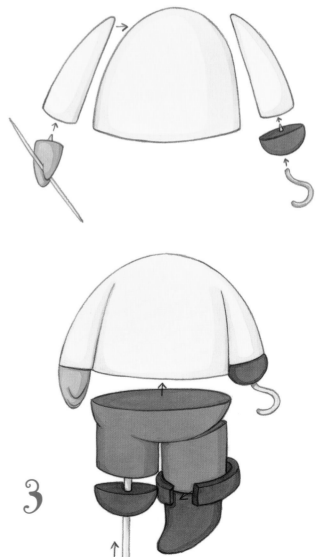

4. Paint stripes on the pants with acrylic paint. Add a modeling clay belt and buckle. For the vest, superimpose rectangles cut from a sheet and just smooth them out over the shoulders.

5. Make the face (see p. 5). Add a black eye patch by flattening a ball over one eye and a thin sausage around his head.

4

5

6

6. Stick the head onto the body and the beard onto the head. You can add little balls so that the beard looks curly. Use the pattern on p. 35 to cut two pieces for the modeling clay hat. Put it on him and paint a skull and crossbones if you like. Stick the pirate onto a modeling clay base.

Don't bother them

Pirates sail all over the world in search of plunder, fighting with anybody who challenges them.

Housekeeper

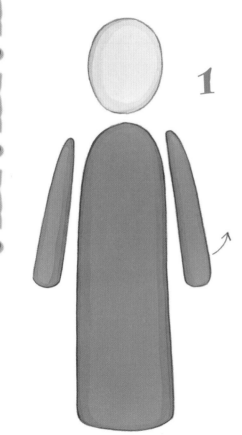

1. A rounded cylinder for the body, two sausages for the arms, and an elongated ball for the head.

2. Make the hands (see p. 5). Join the arms to the body, raising one of them, and smooth the joins. Flatten two balls to make the breasts, thinning them with your thumb.

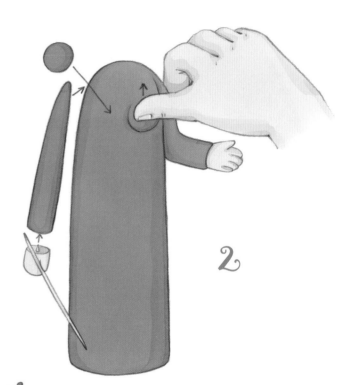

3. Make the face (see p. 5). The eyes should have bags. Make two elongated balls and open a slot in the middle with a toothpick. Fill it with a small white sausage and a little black ball in the center.

Order at home

Housekeepers live and work in large mansions full of mystery. They are always giving orders and are unpleasant.

4. Place a strip of modeling clay around her head and spread it out. Stick a bun on and mark lines to make it look like hair. Stick a ball on the neck and stick the head on top.

5. With the help of a pencil, make a space under the dress to stick two triangles: the shoes. Stick a line of buttons onto the dress.

6. To finish, stick a cardboard key in her hand. Stick a cylinder onto a round base to make a candle and place it in the other hand. Don't forget the modeling clay flame.

Zombie

1. Model a thick cylinder and round it at the top. With the same colored modeling clay, make two sausages for the arms. Two more sausages will make the legs.

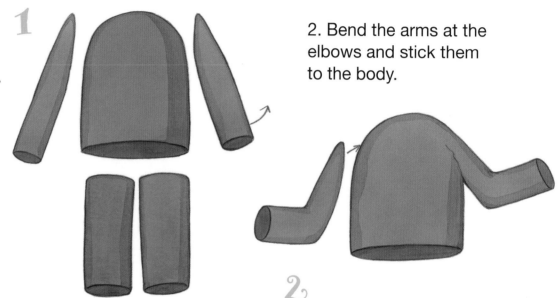

2. Bend the arms at the elbows and stick them to the body.

3. Join the legs together and stick them onto the body. Cut out two long triangles for the jacket collar and mark the jacket line.

4. To make the clothes look old and worn, smooth a little modeling clay from the jacket over the pants. By pressing on a grid, you can simulate patches.

5. The shoes are made from half balls, joined to the pants with a piece of skewer. Model a thick modeling clay base to stick the tips of the skewers in to stand the zombie on. The fingers are made from small pieces of bent wire.

5

Dead or alive?

Zombies are also known as the living dead. They are corpses that emerge from their tombs at night to scare people...

6. Make a poorly mixed ball of cold and white colors for the head. The colored threads simulate the veins. For the eyes, sink in a lilac ball; add another white one and a tiny black one on top. Finish off the face (see p. 5). Stick on the head a bit lopsided. You can paint some blood on his mouth with some nail polish…

6

Spotty

1. Model a cylinder rounded at one end and define the legs. Cut white and colored balls to make the eyes and eyelids. Add a little black ball if you like.

2. Use modeling tools to make a large mouth and perfect it with your fingers. Make a tongue with a triangle of folded construction paper. Make the feet look like they are moving.

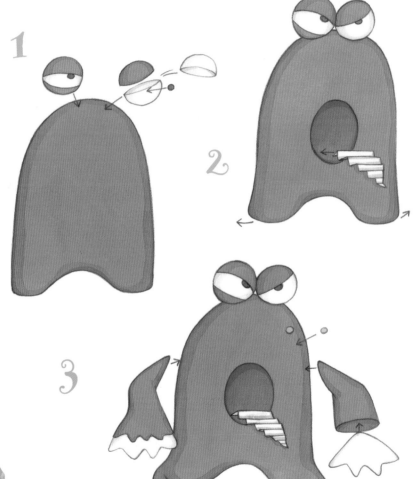

3. Join two construction paper hands to two sausages and spread the modeling clay over them. Stick the arms to the body. Add "spots" with little balls. If he touches you, he will contaminate you!

Patterns

Vampire
Page 12

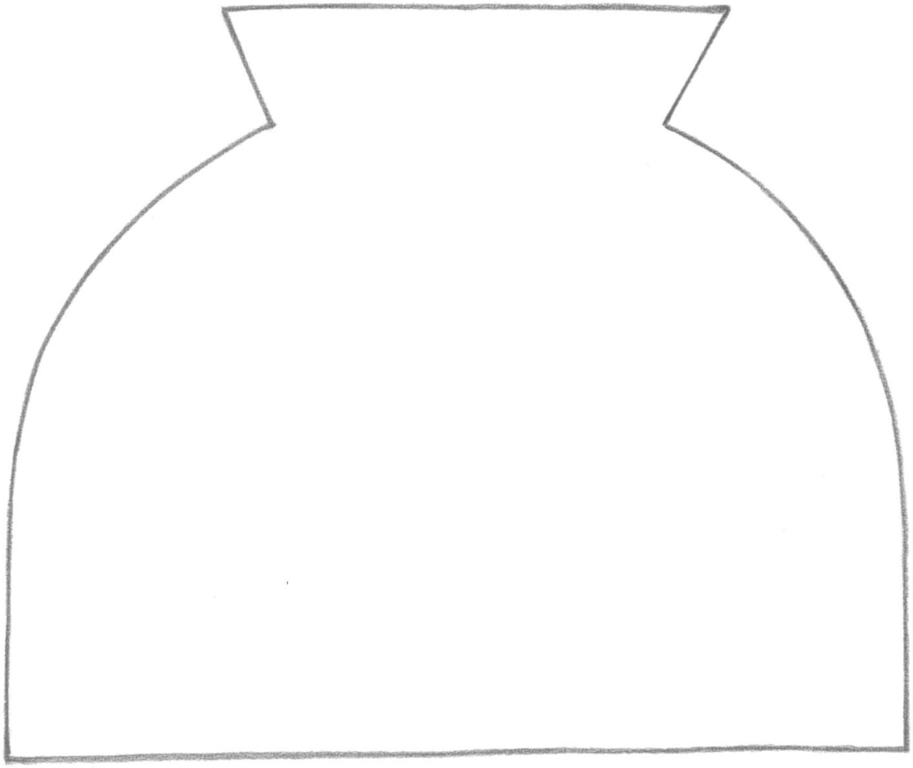

Pirate
Page 28

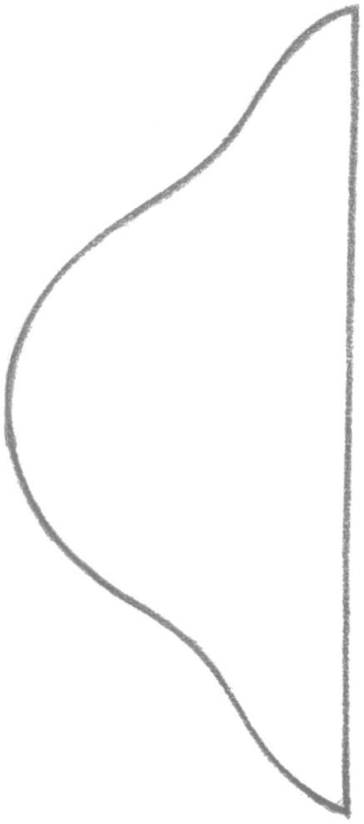

Witch
Page 14

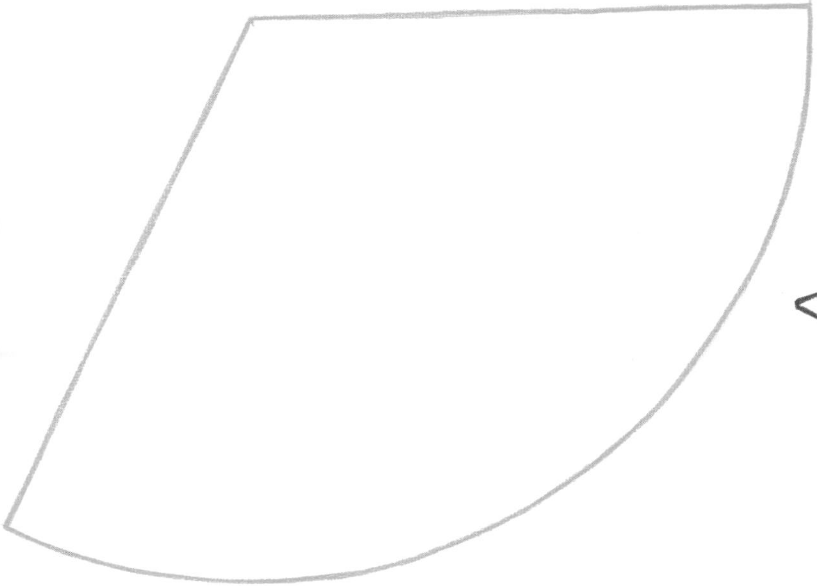

Bat
Page 8

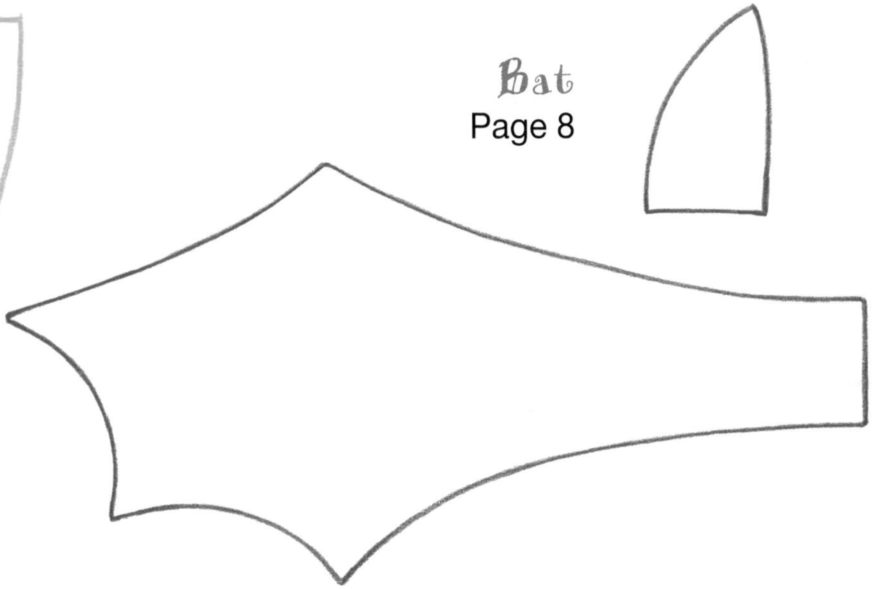

First edition for the United States and Canada published in 2013 by Barron's Educational Series, Inc.

Original title of the book in Catalan: *Modela Personatges de Por*
© Copyright GEMSER PUBLICATIONS S.L., 2013
C/ Castell, 38; Teià (08329) Barcelona, Spain
  (World Rights)
Tel: 93 540 13 53
E-mail: info@mercedesros.com
Website: www.mercedesros.com

Author and Illustrator: Bernadette Cuxart

All inquiries should be addressed to:
Barron's Educational Series, Inc.
250 Wireless Boulevard
Hauppauge, New York 11788
www.barronseduc.com

ISBN: 978-1-4380-0358-0

Library of Congress Control Number: 2013934482

Date of Manufacture: May 2013
Manufactured by: L. REX PRINTING COMPANY LIMITED,
  Dongguan City, Guangdong, China

Printed in China
9 8 7 6 5 4 3 2 1